KHAJURA...

ORCHHA

Text by:

Dr. Rajaram Panda

Published by:
Mittal Publications

Published by Mittal Publications
F-83, Green Park (Main)
New Delhi-110016, India
e-mail: info@mpu.co.in
www.mpu.co.in

Text by Rajaram Panda
Designed by Vipul Jain

Printed by Pritha Offsets Pvt. Ltd.

CONTENTS

PREFACE

Khajuraho after Taj, is the most frequently visited monument in India. Khajuraho is an unique example of Indo-Aryan architecture. It is well known all over the world for its temple architecture and exquisite sculpture. The temples were built between the 9th and 11th centuries by the warrior kings of the Chandela dynasty. It is believed that 85 temples were built out of which 25 still remain in varying degrees of preservation.

Khajuraho is a small village situated along a lake known as the Khajuraho-sagar or Ninoratal in Chhatarpur District of Madhya Pradesh in the heart of central India. It is extended over an area of about 21 square kilometers. The country around Khajuraho is well watered by the Narmada and Chambal, and cradled among hillocks, offshoots of the Panna range which belong to the Vindhya mountains, a natural line of demarcation between north and south India and one of its seven principal mountain chains.

It lies 55 kilometers south of Mahoba, 47 kilometers east of Chhatarpur and 43 kilometers northwest of Panna and is accessible by metalled roads from Mahoba, Harpalpur and Satna railway stations on the Central Railway. The distance from Harpalpur to Chhatarpur is 55 kilometers. There are regular bus-services to Khajuraho from Harpalpur, Chhatarpur, Mahoba and Satna, the last place being 117 kilometers from Khajuraho. There is also a daily air service connecting Khajuraho with Delhi, Agra and Varanasi.

The climate is tropical and the land, which is upland, appears flat and is segmented into basins; in ancient times rainwater was gathered in tanks and bunds it is believed there were sixty-of which there are visible remains. Now there are no more than three large tanks: Khajurasagar, Shiv Sagar and Prem Sagar, used for ceremonial and domestic purposes. The village with a population of about 8,000, most of which lives in mud-houses with clay-tile roofs is now clustered around Khajurasagar, also known as Ninoratal, and is spread over an area that hardly exceeds eight square kilometers. The terrain, dotted with mahua trees whose flowers are used to brew the local liquor, permits intermittent cultivation.

By the sixteenth century, Khajuraho seems to have lost all importance, turning into an obscure village. It remained lost to the outside world until 1838, when Captain T. S. Burt rediscovered the temples. Burt was on official duty, but made a detour from his itinerary to follow the trail that his palki (palanquin) bearer spoke of. He recorded that he had found what was "probably the finest aggregate number of temples congregated in one place to be met in all of India, and in an area within a stone's throw of one another." He copied Dhanga's stone inscription, dated AD 1002, which was lying loose in the Visvanatha Temple.

The very name Khajuraho, according to Alexander Cunningham, has been derived from the word 'Khajoor' the date palm trees. Epigraphic records show that earlier Khajuraho was known as 'Khajurvatika', which means garden of date palms. Date palm trees bearing dates, once clustered round this royal ancient city during its hey days. This view has also been confirmed by the popular belief according to which a pair of gold date palms once adorned the city-gates of Khajuraho.

4

Though the erotic sculptures of Khajuraho are the main attraction to a common visitor to the place and responsible for giving Khajuraho widest publicity and popularity among the tourists, these erotic figures comprise only a part of the entire range of the magnificent sculptures which is full of 'sublime and sensuality'. It should be borne in mind that the Khajuraho sculptures depicting erotic figures are not the 'pornographic scenes to excite savage passion'. The unique sculptures of Khajuraho temples should be seen in totality.

Although Burt wrote that some of the sculptures as extremely indecent and offensive, his work opened Khajuraho to future generations. Years later, Cunningham visited the site and in his 1864 report, counted 872 statues, of which 646 were on the outside walls. He studied other inscriptions, temples, loose images and ruined shrines which had turned into mounds and were scattered through the site, and was struck by the "richness of the carving" and the "profusion of sculptures".

Even that great Victorian puritan Mohandas Karamchand Gandhi, found the temples deeply distressing and gave his blessing to a band of pious vandals who wanted to chip the walls of the temples clean from these "indecent and embarrassing" affronts to their ignorant notions about Indian culture. It took the intervention of no less than Rabindranath Tagore who wrote an appalled letter to Gandhi, explaining that this was a national treasure and could not be so cavalierly demolished because some people were uncomfortable that their ancestors were sexual beings.

Khajuraho, however, continued to be the religious capital of the Chandellas until the fourteenth century. Ibn Batuta, an Arab traveller who visited the area in 1335, describes in his chronicles a place called Kajarra which was inhabited by "jogis with long and clotted hair, their skin yellowed by fasting." He also described, "a great pond, about a mile in length, near which are temples containing idols which the Muslims have mutilated." This lake, now known as Khajurasagar, stands 800 metres east of the western group of temples, which was probably the heart of the old town.

The religious sanctity and sacredness of Khajuraho seems to have some relevance even today among the people in the region, who in large number throng to the place during the Shiv-Ratri festival when a big mela (fair) is held here.

While on the visit to Khajuraho, don't forget to see the Sound and Light Show that is held every evening. The duration of the show is 50 mins. The narrator of the documentary, which is in both Hindi/English, is Amitabh Bachchan, the Great Super Star of India.

Khajuraho Dance Festival is held every spring in the town of Khajuraho in order to celebrate the glory of the temples. It is believed that classical dance basically comes from the Hindu temples and attained it's maturity. This Festival is a cultural festival for the celebration of the Indian arts dance and music handling down from generation to generation..The main idea behind Khajuraho Dance Festival is to make the cultural heritage of Khajuraho relevant to the present society and preserving it for the coming generation. On this occasion a number of renowned artists and craftsmen participates in the workshop and seminar and present their art to the numerous visitors and tourist. And during this seven days festival, there is also a market in an open field where the visitors can get the entire local made articles of Khajuraho. This festival is known not only in our country but also to the outside world at large.

Top right: Acrobatic mouth congress, north wall, Duladeo Temple **Bottom left:** Erotic sculpture, south wall, Duladeo Temple **Bottom right:** Standing congress, Duladeo Temple **Top left:** Standing coitus, Lakshmana Temple.

The Legend of Khajuraho

A panel of dancers flanked by maidens. Khajuraho celebrates the depiction of women in languid postures.

Ancient dynasties are often covered in a veil of mystery, largely because written records are rare and, as is often the case in India, myth and legend weave their way over time into the history of their origin and their reign. And when the dynasty leaves a legacy as contradictory as the Khajuraho temples, with their mix of the religious and the sensuous, the web is woven of brighter threads, the accompanying legends more colourful.

Chandellas are one of the Rajput clans who claim to be the descendants of 'Chandra Kula' (Moon born). The powerful kings of the Chandella dynasty ruled over central part of India for about five centuries beginning from 9th century A.D. Chandellas are famous as the kings of Jejakabhukti what is now a days known as Bundelkhand. The early history of the Chandellas is, however, quite obscure. There are some very interesting myths relating to the origin of the Chandellas.

According to the account of the medieval court poet, Chandbardai, in the Mahoba-khand of his Prithviraj Raso (an epic poem) in the court of Prithviraj Chauhan III (1177-92), ruler of Delhi and Ajmer, Hemavati was the daughter of the family priest of Indrajit, the Gahadwara ruler of Kashi (Varanasi).

The story in brief goes like this. Hemavati was exceptionally beautiful. God Indra, however, got displeased due to one or the other act of this elegant beauty on the earth and by curse of God Indra, Hemavati became widow at the age of sixteen only. One summer night Hemavati experienced strange restlessness. She went to bathe in a near by tank known as 'Rati Talab', which was also known for its lotus. Water in the tank was cool and refreshing. She disrobed and

Standing coitus at Lakshman Temple

Karanavati she would give birth to a son. This son of her would be a mighty king who would extend his kingdom far and wide. The Moon-God also said to her that at the age of sixteen her son would perform a 'yagyan' which would efface her guilt or stigma. After this prophecy the Moon-God disappeared and Hemavati also left her home at Kashi and arrived at Kalinjar. After a few months she gave birth to a son who was extra-ordinary and exceptionally handsome. Chandrama, the celestial father of this newly born male child celebrated the occasion, which was attended by celestial nymphs. The child was named as Chandravarman. Chandravarman grew so robust, bold and a valiant hero that at the age of sixteen he had enough strength to kill a lion and a tiger without any difficulty. Delighted at the bravery and the feats of her son, Hemavati evoked the presence of the Moon-God by reciting hymns. Chandrama descended to the earth, blessed Chandravarman and gave him a touchstone, which could turn iron into gold. As prophesied by

jumped into the water and started swimming leisurely. Chandrama, the Moon-God, got struck when he noticed the dazzling beauty swimming nude in the tank. Chandrama could not resist himself and descended to the earth. They spent the night in passionate consummation. At break of the day as the Chandrama was ready to leave, Hemavati came back to her senses and realized that the Chandrama had ruined her. She became very upset, she was feeling so bad that she threatened to curse the Moon-God. To this, Chandrama smiled and consoled her not to get perturbed and be happy as the offspring of their happy union would be a robust valiant king whose fame and valor would spread all over the world. The effect of this consolation could not last long and the very thought of social stigma horrified Hemavati, she knew not how to conceal her disgrace. In utter helplessness she requested the Moon-God to help her in obliterating her social stigma. Chandrama counseled Hemavati to go to Khajurvatika where on the bank of the river

Nagi queen with a lotus stalk and an apsara painting the wall, Parsvanath temple

8

the Moon-God, Chandravarman became mighty ruler of Mahoba who expanded his territory and built the famous fort of Kalinjara. The Gahadwara ruler of Kashi was overawed by the mighty Army of Chandravarman and surrendered and thus Kashi also became a part of the Chandella kingdom. Thereafter, Chandravarman came to Khajuraho alongwith his queen and performed 'Bhandya Yagyan' to absolve his mother of her stigma. Hemavati desired her son to built eighty-five temples and lakes at the place. Chandravarman fully honoured his mother's wishes and requested the divine builder Vishvakarma to build as many as eighty-five temples. The emblem of the Chandellas became a young man grappling with a lion, a scene on which there is several sculptures at Khajuraho.

According to a variation of this story, which also ascribes to Chandratreya the dynasty of the Chandellas, Hemavati was the daughter of Mani Ram, a priest of the ruler of Kalanjar, eighty kilometers from Khajuraho. On a particular

A maithuna couple, Devi Jagdambi Temple

Apsaras bedecked with ornaments, Duladeo Temple

moonless night, miscalculating the movement of the planets, Mani Ram informed the king that there would be a full moon. When the mistake was discovered, Hemavati, to save her father's reputation, prayed to the moon god to appear; he obliged but, captivated by her beauty, also ravished her. Mortified, Mani Ram cursed himself and turned into stone. In due course, Chandratreya, the begetter of the Chandellas, was born. Maniyadeva, whose shrines still exists at Maniyagadh, nineteen kilometers south of Khajuraho, and Mahoba, came to be worshipped as the family deity of the Chandellas.

Though such (legendary) tales are romantic and interesting, but authorities on this subject consider these tales purely imaginary and believe that these imaginary tales are only to conceal the real origin of the clan. According to R. V. Russell's conjectures, the Bhars, the famous builders in central part of India, were the ancestors of this dynasty. But the Khajuraho stone inscription of Dhanga in 954 A.D. (V. S. 1011) traces the origin of the dynasty to saint

Top: An erotic tantric scene, north wall, Lakshmana Temple **Bottom left:** Maithuna couple from Devi Jagdambi Temple **Bottom right:** An apsara playing with a ball, Lakshmana Temple.

Top: Closeup of plural congress, Kandariya Mahadev Temple **Bottom right:** Brahma with consort Saraswati on south facing niche of Chitragupta Temple **Bottom left:** .A woman playing on a flute, Vishwanath Temple.

Chandratreya. Hence it is believed that 'Chandravarman or Chandratreya was the progenitor of the dynasty. Chandravarman established his capital in Khajuraho and the place remained the capital of his successors too. According to Cunningham, Hemraja, the priest of the Gahadwara ruler Indrajit of Varanasi, was crowned as Chandravarman in 168 A.D. (V.S. 225).

The real historical founder of the Chandella dynasty, according to available evidences, seems to have been 'Nannuka', who ruled in the first quarter of the ninth century A.D. From the earlier inscriptions of Chandella dynasty, it appears that the first few Chandella chief served as feudatories of the Prathiharas. They proclaimed themselves independent when the Prathihara Empire weakened and disintegrated. Nannuka was succeeded by his son Vakpati who ruled during the second quarter of the ninth century. According to one inscription, Vakpati extended his territory and brought some hills of the Vindhyas under his rule. Vakpati had two sons Jaishakti and Vijayshakti, who ruled over the kingdom. Both the princes were brave warriors and they annexed many territories to their kingdom. Jaishakti, who ruled first, was also called Jaijak or Jejaka. Jejaka conferred his name on the region over which he ruled and it came to be known as 'Jejakabhukti'. Jejaka had no son so his younger brother Vijaishakti succeeded him. According to inscriptions Vajaishakti

fought many battles and subjugated a number of neighbouring areas. The exploits and deeds of bravery of Jai and Vijai are often sung in ballads as if the two were joint rulers. Vijaishakti was succeeded by his son Rahil. Rahil ruled over the region for twenty years. Rahilya, village very close to Mahoba at its southwest was named after him. A tank known as Rahilsagar was built and a temple was constructed on its bank. Rahil was succeeded by his son Harshadeva around 900 A.D. Harshadeva ruled for twenty-five years and he has an important place in the history of the dynasty. Harshadeva helped his Prathihara overlord Mahipal I to regain his throne of Kannauj in Oudh, who was invaded and defeated by Rashtrakutas of Deccan. Harshadeva perhaps commemorated this memorable event around 915 A.D. with the building of Matangeshwar temple dedicated to Lord Shiva.

Harshadeva was succeeded by his son Yasoverman also known as Lakshvarman. Yasoverman, however, was the greatest ruler of the dynasty and he was very powerful and fought valiantly the Rashtrakutas of Deccan and Palas of Eastern India. He conquered Kalinjara in the North and extended his kingdom upto Malwa in the south and Ganda and Mithila to the east. He became so powerful that he proclaimed himself an independent king. The Chandellas, during his regime, became great power in the

history of Central India.

Yasoverman was a devout and munificent king and with him begins the era of temple construction by the Chandellas in Khajuraho. Yasoverman built the Lakshmana temple, which was dedicated to Lord Vishnu.

Yasoverman was succeeded by his son Dhanga (954-1002 A.D.) Dhanga like his father stopped paying tributes to the Prathiharas and seems to have finally repudiated the over lordship of Kannauj.

Dhanga further annexed many new areas and expanded his territory. Dhanga assumed the sovereign title of "Maharajadhiraja". Dhanga was not only a great warrior but he was also great builder and lover of art and culture. During his regime two magnificent temples i.e. Vishvanath and Parsvanath temples were built. In fact Dhanga emerged as the most powerful king of North India in the 10th century A.D. Dhanga was succeeded by his son Ganda (1108-1017 A.D.) who ruled only for about nine years. Ganda is said to be the builder of 'Chitragupta' and 'Devi Jagdamba' temples.

Vidyadhara (1017-1029 A.D.) ascended the throne of Khajuraho after the death of his father Ganda. Vidyadhara was a great warrior and a powerful ruler. While he valiantly fought back the Mahmud of Ghazni twice-first in A.D. 1019 and then in A.D. 1022, he subdued the Kalchuris and the Parmaras in the Central India and expanded his kingdom. Under him the Chandella kingdom reached the zenith of its prosperity. He was a great lover of art and culture. The biggest and most elegant temple in Khajuraho, the 'Kandariya Mahadeva' temple was built by him.

Vijaypal succeeded the throne of his father Vidyadhar and somehow managed to retain the territory of his father and also maintained the temple construction actively. 'Vaman' temple is said to have been built by him. Vijayapal was succeeded by his elder son Devavarman who lost some portion of the Chandella territory to Kalchuris. After the death of Devavarman in 1060 A.D. Kirtivarman, brother of Devavarman ascended the throne of Khajuraho who fought many battles and defeated the Kialchuris and got back the Chandella's territories.

Kirtivarman ruled for about forty years and he patronized arts and literature. Famous drama "Prabodh Chandroday" was written at his instance and was also staged before him. A good many temples namely Adinath, Javari and perhaps Chaturbhuja were built during his regime, which ended around 1100 A.D. After Kirtivarman the successors had a very tough time. Their reign was full of wars and battles. The struggle for supremacy in Northern and Central India was in full swing. The Chandella's kingdom was under constant threat of attacks by the Kalchuris and Chalukayas. After Kirtivarman

Plural intercourse, Kandariya Temple **Bottom:** Amorous couple at south-east wall, Devi Jagdambi Temple.

Sallakshan, (also known as Hollakshan), Varman ascended the throne of Khajuraho who was succeeded by his son Jaivarman. Jaivarman suffered a defeat from the Gaharwar ruler, Govind Chandra, in 1120 A.D. and abdicated the throne and started living in a jungle.

Prithvivarman, his uncle, then ascended the throne and somehow protected the kingdom from the enemies. Then Madanvarman, son of Prithvivarman, ascended the throne of Khajuraho in 1130 A.D. Madanvarman was again a brave, valiant warrior in the dynasty, who revived the lost reputation of the Chandellas. Kalinjar, Mahoba, Ajaigarh and Khajuraho were his strongholds. Temple building activities were also seen once again in Khajuraho. The construction of the exquisite temple like 'Duladeo' is attributed to Madanvarman, whose regime ended around 1163 A.D. Madanvarman was succeeded by Yasoverman II who could rule only for two years.

Erotic scene at central row of Kandariya Temple **Bottom:** Amorous couple, Lakshmana Temple.

After the untimely death of his father, Parmardidev ascended the throne of Khajuraho. Parmardidev, the last of the Chandella rulers, ruled for about thirty-five years. The mighty army of Prithviraj Chauhan the famous Rajput king of Delhi attacked Parmardidev. Two brothers, Alha and Udal, the great heroes of Mahoba were the generals of Parmardidev who fought so bravely that their tales of heroic roles and bravery is sung in the area like legendary tales even to this day. 'Alha-udal' is a well-known folklore in Northern India, particularly in Bundelkhand area. In 1182, Paramardideva was defeated by Prithviraj Chauhan. He lost a large chunk of his territory including Mahoba, to him. In 1202, Qutubuddin Aibak, the slave general of Mohammad Ghori invaded Kalanjar. Paramardideva surrendered after a brief struggle, but was put to death by his minister for his cowardice. Subsequently, the Chandella lands came under the grip of the Sultans.

Surasundris or nymphs applying collarium to their eyes. The female figures that embellish the temples are elegant and typically twist around the axis in the tribhanga pose, evoking a languid and sensual air.

Architecture

The ornamental ceilings of the entrance porch of the temples are boldly carved with designs of floral cusps

The group of temples at Khajuraho is a brilliant example of Indo-Aryan style of temple architecture. This large one compact group of temples has certainly some of the finest and most elegant specimen of medieval temple architecture and sculpture in India which are not only fully developed but are also among the best preserved temples. The Khajuraho artist seems to be 'thoroughly versed in the mnemonic traditions and textual canons, the grammar and syntax of architecture and iconography'. According to Benjamin Rowland, "The culmination of the Indo-Aryan genius in architecture was attained in the extra ordinary group of temples erected at Khajuraho in Central India."

The Nagar style of temple architecture is well known mainly for two of its distinct features i.e. the ground plan and the elevation and secondly the cruciform spread and curvilinear spire. The temples of Khajuraho were, except the first temple, i.e. 'Chaunsath Yogini Temple', built of fine-grained sand stone buff pale-yellow and pinkish in colour which were brought from the quarries of Panna on the east bank of river ken. It is said that big stones were carved near the quarries and transported to the site and assembled thereafter and inter-locking system was followed in the entire construction of the temples. Chausath Yogini temple was built in granite stone, but owing to hardness of the local granite stone, the builders and the sculptors had to go for the sand stone from Panna.

Ferguson observed that the Khajuraho temples are so "like one another that it requires great familiarity to distinguish them. It looks as if it all had been built by one prince, and by some arrangement that neither sect should surpass or be jealous of the other. If not under the sway of a

single prince, they must have been erected in an age of extreme toleration." On minute observation and careful study one can find that 'earlier temples contained the simplest symbols or images inside the sanctum, no processional friezes on the mouldings of base and no parallel, horizontal friezes filling the alternate races and projections of the central zone of temple façade'. In Khajuraho arts one can see that there has been greater stress on angular forms with sharp points and edges, on horizontal, verticals and diagonals.

The Shikhara, surrounded by towers seem to be a 'rising crescendo of curves', which ultimately reach the Amalaka, the crowning circular top. The crowning Amalaka is compared to a lotus or a 'solar halo with rays' signifying way to heaven, the summit of the mountain or the skull dome of the universal man'. (Rowland "Art and Architecture of India"). Distinct characteristic of Khajuraho temple architecture is that the temples stand on a lofty terrace and are not surrounded by the usual enclosure walls, proudly proclaiming their presence as if they had nothing to fear from iconoclasts, vandals and marauders. The terrace or the lofty platform provides an outer Pradakshina or open ambulatory on which the devotees can go round the temple. The shrines can be entered into only after ascending a number of stairs, which lead to the portico or Ardha Mandapa. Usually most of the temples, except the Chaturbhuja and Lalgaun Mahadev temples, have their entrance from the east. The above two temples have their entrance from the west.

Percy Brown observes that the entrance or the gateway (Ardha Mandap) are decorated with beautiful 'Toran' which appear like ivory carving. Some of the larger temples, namely the Lakshman, the Kandariya and the Vishwanath temples are known as "Panchayatan" or five shrine temples. 'A Panchayatan temple' comprises of a large central shrine which is the principal shrine housing the deity to whom the temple is dedicated, and four subsidiary shrines at the four corners of the platform which are dedicated to the other members of the panchayat of Gods. The temple structure in general is in five parts, namely Ardha Mandap (the entrance or portico), Mandap (the assembly hall), Antaral (the vestibule), Garbhagriha (the cella or sanctum) and Mahamandap (the transepts) together with Pradakshina path i.e. the circumambulatory passage. Each of these parts has its own decorated artistic roof. Still the peculiarity of these temples is that each temple is a compact architectural unit and not groups of separate constructions or buildings. All these separate structure do not appear as independent structures or buildings but are co-ordinated into a compact architectural synthesis.

The different parts of the temple buildings with series of pronounced mouldings are generally linked in rising gradation, which symbolizes upward urge. Vertically above the lofty terrace are the walls and balconied openings of the interior compartments with two or three parallel bands of sculptures, and above all is the grouping of roofs, culminating in a graceful Sikhara (spire) crowned by the Amalaka (cogged ring stone), which is surrounded by the Stupika (finial) with the Kalas (vase) as its most conspicuous part. 'The balconied window openings, by the scanty light that they admit, help in creating a solemn atmosphere of half light and half darkness, and also break up the otherwise solid mass of the structure.' The Ardha mandaps lighted by oriel windows on both sides. 'The pillared square platform approached by crossing the Ardha mandaps and better known as Mandaps or vedikas also has windows on both sides to let air and light'. In front of the Mandap a few steps ahead is the Garbhagriha (sanctum). Around the Garbhagriha there is the Pradakshina (circumambulatory) passage full of icons chiseled in three successive rows in the temples like Kandariya, Lakshman, Vishwanath and Parashwanath. These are known as 'Sandhara Prasadas' in Hindu temple architecture, which have, a Pradakshina well lighted by big oriel window excepting the Parshwanath Temple, which has two sanctums, one facing the north and the other south. Temples like the Chitragupta, Jagadambi, the Vamana, the Javari, the Duladeo, the Chaturbhuja and the Adinath are known as 'Nirandhara Prasadas' as they have no

Clockwise from top: The statue of Panch Agni at the Lakshman Temple; Shivlinga with images of Shiva, Brahma Temple; Kama with Rati and Preeti at Parshwanath Temple; a dansuse putting bell anklets, Parshwanath Temple.

Clockwise from top: The boar incarnation of Lord Vishnu at Devi Jagdambi Temple ; Yama, the god of death Devi Jagdambi Temple; maithuna couple, Lakshmana Temple; an emblem of the Chandela dynasty .

A surasundari (celestial nymph) painting the sole of the foot, Parsvanath Temple.

principal from ribs, converging in one overlapping rush to the top. These peaks are punctuated by globular kalashas or pitchers and by pointed Bijswaras or 'seedsounds'. The rhythmic term of the rounded base of the attendant peaks harmonizes with the bulbous shape of their grooved heads. These are accompanied by parallel bands and necking, fillets and inter spaces, full of light and shadows. The main salient of the façade usually ascend up to a point and then shed their outward curves to bend inwards. The pillar capitals are actual pillars supporting roofs. Some times they are squat and bare without sculptured brackets. Some are tall and elegant, decorated with beaded, interlacing, half circular garlands, intersected in turn, by bells and chains, dangling from Kirtimukhas or mythical faces of glory. Equipped with an octagonal base and a cylindrical top, they carried bracket consoles for holding Shalabhanjikas (woman sporting with trees), Jain Tirthankaras, and other figures mortised in sockets." (K. Chakravarty). The interiors of the temples were designed strictly according to the

Pradakshinas. The separate pyramidal roofs of the four structures rise in a regular gradation from the lowest over the Ardhamandap to the loftiest of the Garbhagriha. This rising gradation symbolizes an upward urge. Benjamin Rowland says "the dominant impression of Khajuraho shrines is that of number of separate super-structures, each with its Amalaka and finial, building up to a great mountain of masonry. The verticalism is emphasized throughout from the high base through the successive walls and roofs to the ultimate range of lesser peaks that constitute the main spire." The grace and upward thrust of these Shikharas is accentuated by rendering the rhythmic disposition of the main curves and the subtle distribution of miniature turrets (urusringas) clustered all round the main Shikharas (Mulamanjari). The super structure or the Shikhara above the bigger assembly-hall ends just below the 'Sukanasa' (Parrot pillar). 'The Sukanas' is the last halting point.' " A lion overlooks the peak of the main tower from its base. The main Shikhara or the summit now rises, like a

A nymph showing lover's nail marks, Lakshman Temple.

22

requirements of the ritual. In a temple with the inner circumambulatory passage, there exists another pair of transepts with window openings round the sanctum and a third opening in the rear to illumine the passage. A shallow passage (Antarala) with a large moon-stone-step (Chandrasila) leads up to the ornate doorway of the sanctum. The two or three bands of sculptures all round the exterior of the temple and outside the sanctum (Antarabhitti), following the alternate projections (Rathas) and recesses (Salilantara) of the walls, portray, besides the figures of the principal Gods and Goddesses, Ashtadikapalas (the regents of the eight quarters) Apsaras and Sura-sundaris (celestial nymphs) Mithunas (couples), Vidyadharas (flying celestials), Nagas (serpents), Sardulas (leografis) etc. In the words of Chakravarty, "the mature Khajuraho style was distinguished by axial integration, elevation on open and high platform, by inner ambulatory and outer promenade, by ornamental basement moldings and walls, varied by balconied dromerstyle windows, by double cross ground

A surasundari applying vermilion on the forehead, Lakshman Temple

plan, curved ceilings and triple plastic griddles, the decorative splendour of this style was derived not from external appendages but from the fine grained sandstone of varying shades and tones. The gradually accentuating crescendo of the stupendous tower, the use of delicately decorated columns for wall-spacing and corner resolution, the chiaroscuro of light and shade created by the changing texture of the recesses and projections and the exceptionally elegant three quarter profiles and back views of the view figure sculptures which blended with and enhanced the architectural pile gave a special and inimitable flavour to the Khajuraho style. Ultimately, in Khajuraho, temple architecture was a marvel of the perfectly evolved Nagra style in which the counter pointed melodies of architecture and sculpture were held in a fine tune complex balance." The sculptor's fine skill and a sense of imagination have given form to human emotion in the form of spiritual and physical love.

A nymph applying sindoor, Lakshman Temple.

The female figures that embellish the temples are elegant and typically twist around the axis in the tribhanga pose, evoking a languid and sensual air.

Sculptures

Seen from any angle, the temple walls are alive with sculptures, a meritorious feat for the medieval sculptor who worked with little more than his chisel and imagination to create these marvellous works of art.

Khajuraho sculpture is the brilliant illustration of Hindu iconography. Enormous, gracious and fascinating images of varied categories have been lavishly chiseled both on the interior and exterior walls of the huge mountain-like temples of Khajuraho. The walls of the temples are so profusely sculptured that the entire construction, for a while, appears to be a single heavily carved, piece. No space on the walls of some of the temples has been left without significant sculptures. One can count as many as 872 images or statues of 2½ft. to 3 ft. in height on the walls of the Kandariya temple, 674 on the Vishwanath temple. On the body of the Varah in Varaha temple 672 figures of Hindu Gods and Goddesses have been carved. The patient hands of the craftsmen have transformed even the mundane to excellence, depicting a maiden stretching her limbs in the morning, another wringing water out

of her hair after a bath, and a Surasundari taking out a thorn out of the sole of her foot. Such detail in these sculptures, like the depiction of strained muscles and cuts on the calf muscles or the biceps is unparalleled anywhere else in the world. Besides erotic sculptures there are court scenes and scenes of battle and advice to the citizens of the kingdom.

The mass of these stone edifices, countered by intricate carvings, would appear lavish but the sculptures were alternated with linear patterns etched in deep hollows between them, which allowed space. Kaimur sandstone, which was largely used in the Khajuraho temples, was most receptive to chiseling and allowed the sculptors to carve minute details like folds of garments, ornaments, drops of water, strands of hair, nails and creases of the skin. The Hindu ideal of beauty is formalized, and images made for worship were

The sculptures that adorn the temple facades and interiors focus on the world of divinity, of women and of mankind, their portrayal bridges the twin realms of real and the ideal.

The temples of Khajuraho are renowned for their depiction of human passion in stone, and this is an example of the large body of erotica placed on the temple walls.

Depiction of Agni with Swaha at Parsvanath Temple

masterpieces of medieval India.

The profusely carved figures on the walls of Khajuraho temples have been classified broadly into five categories.

The first category comprises formal cult images executed almost completely in the round, in strict conformity with canonical formulae & prescriptions. The images of principal deities like Shiva, Vishnu, Surya and Jain Tirthankaras, which were carved strictly in accordance with the canonical rules, and housed in the inner sanctum of the temples.

The second category is of divinities, minor Gods and Goddesses, Apsaras and Sura-sundaris (celestial nymphs) mainly caved on the interior bands and in the pillared niches. While some of these figures have been carved in high relief, others have been carved in medium relief and yet some figures have been carved in the round. These relief-sculptures present three-dimensional effect. The Nayikas of the Khajuraho

in accordance with the canons laid down in the Shilpashatras: the face is required to be "rounded like a hen's egg", the forehead is compared to a bow, the eyes are usually long and tapering, shaped like a fish, the eyebrows are likened to the leaves of a Neem tree, the chin to a mango stone, the hands and feet to lotus flowers, the waist is slender like a wasp's, while the breasts and hips surge to roundness.

The Khajuraho builders employed corbelling, projecting horizontal blocks of stone to support vertical structures, which produced roofs like leveled domes; cement and mortar were rarely used. Sculptures were contiguous with architecture. Each slab of stone or granite was chosen, sanctified and carved before it was placed in its allotted space and any stone which got damaged would be discarded as it was considered inauspicious. The Khajuraho builders worked in an inspired flood of creativity and the sculptures, which conform to the classical traditions, are among the

A couple with a monkey, north wall, Lakshman Temple.

temple art are enchanting beauties who got their proportionate fleshy body from the chisel of their creator, that is, the master craftsman and these Nayikas fully conscious of their youth and beauty stand in varied provocative postures and display their contours and curves of the fleshy, flexible gracious limbs in coquettish manner, they deliberately display their nudity to attract the onlooker or the passerby. The Master artist has not only chiseled the fleshy body contours, excellent turns and twists and postures of these Nayikas but their erotic moods, sentimental facial expressions, provocative and seductive gestures have also been clearly made visible with the storkes of his artistic chiseling. These celestial and elegant beauties sometimes can be seen as attendants of deities where they are with folded palms, carrying lotus flowers for offering to the deity, sometimes holding mirrors, sometimes applying collyriums to the eyes, sometimes wrings her wet hair after bath and water falls in driblets (Vishwanath), sometimes extracting

Vishnu Laxmi, southern wall, Parshwanath Temple.

thorn from her foot, sometimes yawning or disrobing or touching the breasts. Some time she picks up her foothold it with her delicate and slim fingers and with another hand she paints the foots with Mehandi that is henna. She is playful plays with ball, plays a flute, dances with ecstasy, opens her lips to sing, holds a pen in one hand and a page of paper in another to write a letter, absorbed in thinking puts her pen in her mouth, frets in gloom and despair. Thus woman in maximum range of her form and moods found most important place in the Khajuraho sculpture. Woman occupied so much importance that some scholars could not help saying that woman is the theme of Khajuraho art. Perhaps to the Khajuraho artist, who might have also been a great thinker and a philosopher of his time, woman symbolized the creative energy the Shakti, and depicted in his art in various form such as river, mother Goddesses, Apsaras, Sursundaris or Nayikas, Shalabhanjikas, dancer or even as ordinary woman engrossed in secular activities.

Surasundaris from Adinatha Temple

The third category, comprises of Mithunas that is couples engaged in sexual orgies. Sexual congress demonstrated in the temple art of Khajuraho is most stimulating and open ways to many controversies, yet these depictions of sexual acts are the sources of main attraction and most of the tourists visit Khajuraho to have a look of these unique sexual congress, nudity, bestiality in variety of poses. The sexual acts depicted on the walls of the Khajuraho temples exhibit 'Rati Krida' or love sport with many of its forms and aspects. "The couples execute gymnastic or unnatural poses described in texts like Kamasutra, Rati Rahasya, Ananga Ranga. They fornicate in standing sitting, supine, side and reverse positions. They engage in oral sex extra-vaginal or autoerotic sex. The lady mounts the man like mounting a tree (Lakshman, Parshwanatha). She bends and stands on all fours on the ground like a cow while the man performs from behind (Duladeo and Kakshman). She engulfs a man in a coital embrace like a creeper embraces a tree. The main performer stands on his or her head, supporting other (Kandariya, (Vishwanath). The make picks up and supports the girl on his thighs by flexing his necks, while the lady wraps her arm around his neck (Kandariya). A man has sex with a mare (Lakshman)." (K. Chakravarty). 'Nude male and female showing genital organs, or touching one another private part while embracing' is yet another form of erotic sculpture. Sexual congress in-group or plural intercourse wherein four persons participate with one woman, or three women with one man is another type of erotic sculpture in Khajuraho temples. In one of depictions under this category there is a scene where "a male stands on his head and enjoys three woman simultaneously, one seated on him and two flanking him and helping him in the act. In the other, the position is reversed. While the lady stands on her head, the male partner takes her position.' In another group of erotic sculpture, depicted scenes of 'coitus between human beings and animals. Such images can be seen in Vishwanath, Kandariya and Lakshman temples. In some scenes a lady is shown cohabiting with an animal, while in others it is the man who is shown in union with a beast." (V. P. Seth) Two more interesting features of the erotic sculpture in Khajuraho are (a) 'presence of a third party with the cohabiting couples in some case, (b) 'the erotic coitus figures have invariably been shown in standing poses'. Yet another group of erotic sculpture comprises of, though comparatively very few in numbers, Ascetics in sexual orgies.

In Lakshman temple 'an ascetic is depicted standing with club in an autoerotic pose near an aristocratic couple. Another representation of such a motif is on the Vishwanath temple in which an ascetic is seen copulating with a woman from the rear'. In this process of depicting varied modes and postures of sexual orgies, there are autoerotic scenes where 'attendants, while assisting the main couple, are often shown touching their own sexual parts in many temples of Khajuraho'.

In the fourth category, the sculpture depicts group of dancers and musicians, hunting scenes, animal fight, army marching, sculptor at work, teacher teaching his pupils and several other

secular scenes depicting activities of contemporary period. This category consists of thin friezes of carvings in relief of varying depths.

The fifth or the last category consist of sculptures of animals including the vyala or sardula, which is heraldic and fabulous beast, primarily represented as a rampant horned lion with an armed human rider on the back and a warrior counter-player attacking it from behind. Numerous varieties of this basic type are known with heads of elephant, man, parrot, boar etc. Like the Apsaras, this is the most typical and popular sculptural theme of Khajuraho and is similarly invested with a deep symbolism. Temples of Khajuraho are classified into two groups on the basis of erotic motifs. The first group consists of Lakshman, Kandariya Mahadeva, Devi Jagadambi temple, Chitragupta temple and Vishwanatha temple. In this group of temples

sculptures depicting erotic scenes have been exhibited in abundance and in prominence. Erotic scenes in prominence can be seen on the outer walls, on the recessed parts of the temples, on the cornice and even inside the sanctum.

The second group of temples consists of the Chaturbhuja, Parswanatha, Adinath, Javari, Vamana and Duladeo temples. The construction period of these temples are between 1050 A.D. to 1150 A.D. Erotic motifs displayed in this group of temples are comparatively fewer. Of course Duladeo temple consists of enormous copulating scenes, quite a number of them in gymnastic poses. Javari and Vamana temples though display a few copulating scenes but they are not very aggressive, where as in Adinath and Chaturbhuja temples absence of erotic motif is a striking feature.

Features of Khajuraho Sculptures

The foremost features of Khajuraho sculpture are unique harmonization of architecture and sculpture. In Khajuraho temples architecture and sculpture went hand in hand. In the words of Stella Kramrisch, "The figures seem to resile charged with energy from the surface which they touch and not only from that of the wall of the temple but from any surface, be it one of their own body."

The grace and liveliness in the figures is the outcome of 'Anga-Nyasa', what Stella Kramrisch indicates by saying "sense of touch which was given a training and purpose of the highest order in ancient India." It is 'Anga-Nyasa' treatment, which is attributed to be responsible for making the Khajuraho, sculptures a rare specimen of art in India. 'The erect stance of the images where the weight of their bodies is equally divided is known as Sambhanga, the slight bend as Abhang. The triple bend Tribhanga and the excessive triple bend as Atibhanga, falling under these categories of poses women are shown standing, facing front, side or back'.

The Gods wearing fluttering garments and special type of jewellery make them fit for dancing and flying and add to their dignity and elegance. In the worlds of Stella Kramrisch 'Garments, jewellery and coiffure of the images are a selection and enhancement of those worn in the respective country where the temple was built." Dhoti worn by the figures clings so closely to the body that 'it can be discerned only where its hem is carved on the limbs. The greater Gods wear crowns or Mukutas, which add to their heights. While the lesser ones only wear chignons at the back of their heads which by their various shapes add balance and proportion to the images.'

The greatest and the unique feature of the Khajuraho Sculpture is Dynamism in static, action and movement in immovable. Sculpture commonly known as the art of static depicting one mood or movement or postures only. But at Khajuraho the sculptures and figures are dynamic and they appear to be in action and movement. In Duladeo temple a battle scene is illustrated where horses, elephants and men rush tumultuously into battle; men and animals scamper away to clear the way of the army men.

The frieze from Lakshmana Temple depicts the start of sexual intimacy between a couple.

In the right outside small frieze of the Kandariya temple there is an impressive scene depicting a king on horseback attacking a lion with the double-edged sword held in his right hand. He is holding the horse's reign in his left hand and is looking back at the lion, which is trying to attack him from the back. The lion has placed his front paws on the loin of the horse. Another such scene illustrates a man kneeling with a bow stretched and aiming a shot at a boar in front. The boar is shown in leaping postures, with his front legs held high up in the air. The poor animal knows not how to escape the fatal aim. Hunting scenes would seem to support the view that animals were killed not for their skins only but also for their meat, because the most common animals of the hunt were the deer and the boar whose flesh is relished.

The Vidyadharas fly with scimitar, slicing the sky, their bodies tense arches, their eyes bulging, and nostrils trembling. Singers sing absorbed,

A lady pulling out a thorn from her foot, Kandariya Mahadev Temple

their mouths formed into an O, putting their hands over their ears (Vishwanatha). In Vishwanatha temple another such interesting scene depicts 'two men, tipsy and merry, greedily receive the wine bowl from a man and try to drag an unwilling and unreformed puritan to join the club. Their delight in communal cup is dynamically communicated by a few gestures. In Parshwanath Temple one scene depicts a very sick man with his prominently visible ribs and sunken chest taking advice from a physician'. (K. Chakravarty).

Chakravarty aptly observes that 'Even the individual images or couples are instinct with movement. Even when the couples do not obviously incline towards or approach each other and even when the individual figures are frozen immobile in a stance, they quiver with arrested and potential movement. They station themselves on an axis, taking the naval as the center, the spinal cord as the vertical medium. From this physical and psychic center of perfect equipoise and gravitational balance, they go from the minimum to the maximum deviations. They rotate, exploring the circumscribed space within the periphery of a circle, vertically, horizontally or obliquely. The deflections of the body from the central plumb-line or the movements of the hands are now tentative and now in the round, trying to reach, in space and time, the movement of the most rapturous, dynamic balance'.

Smaller or miniature figure alongside a bigger one depicts the element of perspectivity. There are a number of illustrations in the temples of Khajuraho and some panels preserved in the museum, where small male or female figure is shown standing to one or the other side (at a distance) of the main figure. The smaller figure appears to be that of a servant or an attendant. To denote the difference and the distance (in status and class as well) between the two figures, the Khajuraho artist might have utilized this technique. For example, a woman applying collyrium to her eyes and behind her at some distance showed a male, perhaps an admirer of

The impossible postures are probably a vertical representation o a plural intercourse that would take place on a horizontal plane.

Subjects of everyday life have been adroitly dealt with in the friezes around the temples.

the lady, who is watching the operation. Now smaller size of a full grown man as compared to that of the woman could only have been depicted to mark the distance between the performer and the watcher. (Parshwanath Temple). The Parshwanath Temple has yet another illustration of the perspective leement. A dancer while getting ready for performing her show is fastening 'Ghunghru' (ring-bells) in one of her legs, while a helper woman is shown standing with another set of Ghunghrus in her hands. The portrait of the helper woman is smaller in size. Not only the different sizes of these portraits but their postures, gestures and dresses too suggest the relationship between the two figures and illustrate the perspective. A museum panel showing a young farmer with his sickle tied on the hip is standing with his hands folded in the 'Anjali Mudra'. An elderly man is shown standing at some distance from him.

Another striking feature of the Khajuraho sculpture is portrayals of 'Vahanas' (Vehicle) of Gods and Goddesses. All Hindu Gods and Goddesses have their Vahanas or vehicles and various animals and birds serve the purpose of Vahanas. Vahanas of Gods and Goddesses usually by their sides have been shown in smaller size. Rat is the vahana of Lord Ganesha and Nandi (bull) is the vahana of Lord Shiva. The sculptor has very skilful conveyed various expressions, such as love, astonishment through their looks, and he did it by turning the eyes and the erect ears. For example, Nandi (bull) of Shiva looking at him fondly, with devotion or astonished in his Tandava Nritmurti or Ugramurti. In the museum, the Rat of Ganesh showed bearing joyous expressions to its master. Mostly the Vahanas, standing by the sides of their masters in satiety and placid mood as if they were fully aware of their roles and they also are 'convinced about the fair and confidence their masters have in them'.

In the words of Dr. U. Agarwal, "Khajuraho art seems to have a specific place of its own in the history of Indian sculpture. They constitute rare specimens of our later medieval art, and exhibit to perfection the dynamism, and the sensuous vitality that distinguish the art of this period from that of Saranath. Khajuraho Sculptures, however, exhibit a range of design, form, and expressions to be found neither in the art of the Gupta age, nor even in the contemporary temples at Bhubaneswar. It would thus appear that the Khajuraho sculptures mark a definite stage in the evolution of this art in India.

Erotic Sculptures : Sensual and sublime.

The erotic sculptures of Khajuraho are really a great enigma. The erotic figures carved on the walls of the Khajuraho temples, on the one hand create engrossing interest and on the other hand they provoke a good deal of controversy. The question as to why obscene and erotic figures should be there in a place meant for worship and religious congregation oscillates each and every visitors' mind or even one who hears about Khajuraho temples. In fact the splash of sexual acts and erotic figures on the walls of the Khajuraho temples is considerably responsible for the great interest in the Khajuraho Temples.

Khajuraho temples are the juxtaposition of religion and sex. The depiction of obscene or sexual figures on the walls of the temples is a general feature of medieval Indian temple sculpture. Such scenes can be seen on the walls of many other temples of ninth, tenth and eleventh centuries. But the scenes on the walls of Khajuraho temples, of course, depict the sensuous pleasures of life in exaggerated manner. It is said that the structure as a whole is symbolic in itself and signifies that 'like our bodies, in which the soul, the real source of life, dwells inwards and is immune from the garishness of the flesh, so also the central image of the deity, enshrined in the sanctum has no sculptural decorations about it. Our senses should in fact be directed inwards where there is only Purushottama or the God Supreme.'

Just as the evil deeds attract evildoers, so godliness attracts the Gods. Gods like Indra and Varuna are the masters of natural calamities like

A couple shown kissing, Chitragupta Temple

experience in the Buddhist Tantric temple of Tibet, "when the Lama has reached the stage of spiritual training where he thinks he can look upon the flesh without emotions or without being moved by such sights he enters the 'obscene Idol House' for self examination, where extremely life-like figures depicted in most lewd postures are intended to test the full self control that he has achieved. Besides, beautiful women, especially trained in the arts and wiles of womanhood

begin to dance before him. The Lama sits in the Buddha's Bhumisparsha Mudra studying his own reactions. If he remains unmoved, he has certainly conquered his senses, if he not, he will again have to prepare himself for this 'post-graduate' examination".

Kalinjar, the fortified city near Khajuraho was a big center of Tantric practices. Tantrics believed in amalgamation of sex into religion and stressed on sexual practices as religious ritual. This doctrine of Tantrics seems to be based on ancient or

cyclones and lightning. Temples being abodes of Gods will attract Indra, Varuna and all other Gods, But they seeing the obscene scenes depicted all round, will leave the place in utter aversion and hence the temples will remain secure.'

Another probable reason is that these erotic figures have been carved to test the sincerity and concentration of the devotees. The devotee will stand unmoved at the sight of these obscene if they are sincere. If not, they will yield to their senses and leave the temple without going up to the sanctum and bowing down before the deity; as one can reach to the sanctum only after attaining control of senses.

The origin of the obscene figure on the walls of the temples of medieval India is also traced to the Tantric Form of Buddhism. In Tibet, the Buddhist devotees who wanted to enter their monasteries were required to pass through this test. According to Harrison Foreman, who gave account of his

A maithuna group from Kandariya Mahadev Temple

Surasundaris form a favourite theme at Khajuraho. They are a manifestation of the artists imagination depicting feminine grace and sensuousness.

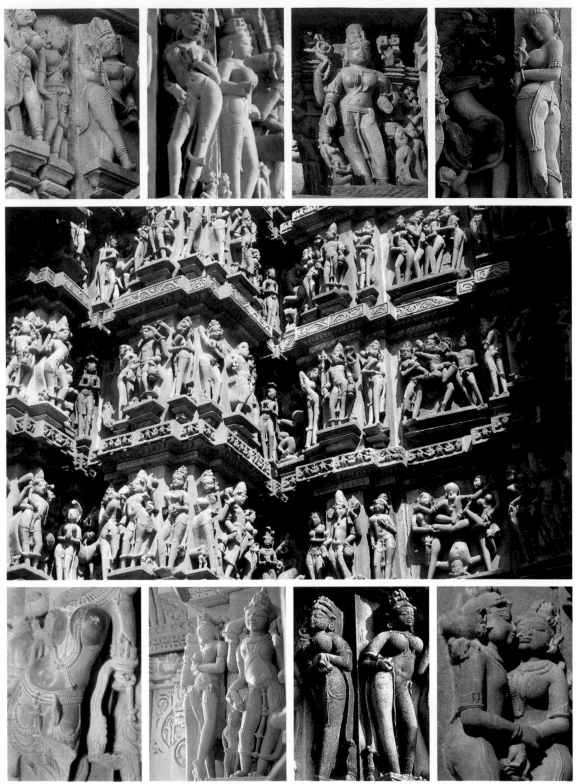

The chisels of the finest craftsmen have created a rhythmic movement through varied activities, further accentuating the feminine grace.

A maithuna couple, north wall, Vishwanath Temple.

primitive fertility rites practiced not only in India but all over the world. In some of the medieval churches in European countries figures of nude female Goddesses have been depicted. It is said that phallic worship was prevalent in ancient Babylon, Egypt, Greece, Italy, U.S.S.R. and some other East European countries.

In the words of Mulkraj Anand, "the erotic sculpture in the medieval temples did not spring up suddenly through the perversity of some local Raja." Sex life, in fact, had been viewed as a sacred tie, right from the days as old as Rigvedic period. Importance of sex in life, as laid down in Veda, can be understood from the fact that out of the total five hundred and thirty six hymns in the Atharva Veda as many as forty one hymns are about sex only. A couplet of the Brihadarnyaka Upnishada states, "In the embrace of his beloved a man forgets the whole world everything both within and without, in the very same way, he who embraces the self knows neither within nor without." Once the sexual motif was accepted in the sculptural scheme of the temple and had been established in the canon, erotic art became a motif by itself.

Sexo-yogic technique is attributed to be an important method in Tantrism for attaining non-dual state or nirvana. In tenth century Matsyendra Nath founded his school of 'Yogini Kaula'. This cult states "Kaula Marga" is the path of controlled enjoyment of sense objects because yoga and Bhoga are one." The oldest temple in Khajuraho is said to be the "Chausath Yogini Temple" which might have been the seat of this sect.

As the true aesthete, the Khajuraho artist never went for mere enjoyment of the body without reaching for the soul. He exalted sexual pleasure as the joy nearest to the ecstasy in realization of God. It is the essence of joy of life, made of 'Rasa' and 'Rati', exaltation, physical and mental, Raga, and Vega, love overflowing the soul and the body.

Sringara Rasa or sensual enjoyment was the high road to joy supernal, or an auspicious motif of temple decoration. No temple was complete without description of 'Mithunas' or couples in Lokalila or worldly sport. Even in Vedas 'Dyaus' and 'Prithvi', the heaven and the earth are regarded as parents of the universe. Mithuna was an important element in the overall decoration and prepared them for union".

Sex was not a stigma or a forbidden thing in the society, which the artist of Khajuraho lived in. The erotic sculptures in and outside the walls of the temples were the requirement of the time, it had the approval of the society and sanctions of the religion. So the erotic sculptures on the walls of the Khajuraho temples has religious sanctity and philosophical background. Hence instead of considering these erotic sculptures as vulgar or obscene, they should be taken as the ecstasy, the beauty and the truth.

A maithuna frieze, north wall, Vishwanath Temple.

41

Clockwise from top left: An illuminated Vishwanath Temple; details of Kandariya Mahadev Temple; Chausath Yogini Temple; a sunset view of Kandariya Temple and Devi Jagdambi Temple; Vishwanath Temple; Javari Temple.

42

The Temples of Khajuraho

The elegant Lakshmana Temple is the best preserved of the evolved temples at Khajuraho.

Temples are the abodes of the divinities or Gods. The Khajuraho temples are not affiliated to any particular sect. These temples were dedicated mainly either to Shiva or to Vishnu or to the Jain Tirthankaras. As per tradition, eighty-five temples existed at Khajuraho, of which hardly one fourth is left now. For convenience these temples are divided into three broad groups, viz, the Western Group, the Eastern Group and the Southern Group.

The Western Group

The western group of temples, in a beautiful park, which the visitor encounters first, is situated along the Bamitha-Rajnagar road to the west of the Khajuraho village and north of the Shiv-sagar Tank. This is the largest and most important group with most of its constituent temples laid out roughly in two rows. The monuments of the western group, enclosed by a fence, are open to public daily between sunrise to sunset on payment of a nominal admission fee.

This closely packed group is believed to cover what was originally a sacred lake, and contains almost all the larger temples of Khajuraho, with the exception of Parvanatha and Duladeo. Two of these, the Lakshmana and the Vishvanatha, are specifically recorded to have been built by kings, while a third, Kandariya Mahadeva that is the most spectacular temple of Khajuraho, was obviously a royal construction. The larger temples of this group face east and run north south in two parallel rows on opposite sides of the park. All the temples of this group are Shiva or Vaishnava, except the Chitragupta temple, which is the only Sun temple at Khajuraho.

1. Chausath-yogini Temple (late 9th century)

The Chausath-yogini temple, made of coarse

Matangeshwar Temple, built in c. AD 900-25.

granite is the earliest building at Khajuraho and is situated on a low granite outcrop to the southwest of the Shiva-Sagar tank. The temple has an exceptional plan and design. Standing on a lofty (5.4 metres high) platform, it is an open-air quadrangular (31.4 m by 18.3 m) structure of sixty-seven peripheral shrines, of which only thirty-five have now survived.

The shrines are tiny cells, each entered by a small doorway, and are severely plain and roofed by a curvilinear sikhara of an elementary form. The shrine in the back wall, facing the entrance, is the largest and constitutes the main sanctum. A few simple moldings on the façade are all the decoration that the temple displays, but in spite of its uncouth appearance and rugged bareness, it possesses an elemental strength and reveals some basic traits of the Khajuraho style, such as a lofty platform and a Jangha (wall) divided into two registers. This temple belongs to Sakti cult.

The three surviving images, representing Brahmani, Mahesvari and Mahishasura-mardini, are massive and squat in form and are among the oldest sculptures of Khajuraho. The latter two are inscribed as Mahesvari and Hinghalaja. The evidence of the sculptural and of the short labels on the images indicates that the temple is probably datable to the last quarter of the ninth century.

2. Lalguan-Mahadeva Temple (c. AD 900)

This temple, situated 803 m west of the Chausath-yogini, is built on the bank of an old lake, called Lalguan-sagar. Built of granite and sandstone, this shrine is now in ruins. It is a structure of modest size and design roofed by a dilapidated pyramidal superstructure of receding tiers of Pidhas. Its entrance-porch has completely disappeared and the doorway is plain but for a diamond carved on the doorsill.

It belongs to the transitional phase when sandstone was introduced but granite had not ceased to be used. It stands on high granite Jagati,

Kandariya Mahadev Temple, built in c. AD 1025-50.

while sandstone was introduced for the Shikhara, only parts of which still stand. At the outside in front of the entrance the broken image of Nandi is still there. This is one of the two temples facing west. This was dedicated to Shiva and supposed to have been built in 900 A.D.

3. Varaha Temple (c. AD 900-925)

The Varaha shrine, built on a lofty plinth, is essentially similar in design to the Lalguan-Mahadeva, but is simpler and more modest. It is an oblong pavilion with a pyramidal roof of receding tiers, resting on fourteen plain pillars, and enshrines a colossal monolithic image of Varaha incarnation of Vishnu in the animal form. The Varaha or boar image in the shrine is 8'9" long and 5'9" high carved of a single block of stone. All over the body of the boar some 672 figures of Hindu Gods and Goddesses are carved.

The serpent Seshanag is pedestal, which also preserves the feet of the broken figure of the earth goddess (Prithvi). Its flat ceiling is carved with an

Jatkari or Chaturbhuj Temple, built in c. AD 1100.

exquisite design of lotus flower in relief. The shrine is built entirely of sandstone. It is obviously later than the Brahma and Lalguan-Mahadeva temples, which belong to the phase of transition between granite and sandstone, and is assignable to circa 900-925.

4. Matangesvara Temple (c. AD 900-925)

This is the only temple in worship in Khajuraho. It is dedicated to Shiva. There is a huge linga in the Garbhagriha made of highly polished colossal stone of 3'8" in diameter and 8'4" high. A large Gauripatta 20'4" in diameter and 4'5" high in which the linga is set occupies the entire floor of the sanctum. This is a plain square temple, which is 24½ ft. square internally and 35 ft. square externally with oriel windows on three sides. The temple faces east direction where the projecting portico is there with a number of steps leading to a high sanctum.

On plan and is design, it is a grand elaboration of the Brahma temple, which this notable difference

Vishwanatha Temple, built in AD 1002.

that the central projections on the three sides are marked by balconied windows, canopied by projecting caves, which are so characteristic of the developed Khajuraho temples.

Since both its exterior and interior are almost plain and devoid of the exuberant sculptured and carved ornamentation, which came to be a hallmark of the developed Khajuraho style, there is no doubt that this is one of the developed Khajuraho style, there is no doubt that this is one of the earliest temples of Khajuraho, assignable to circa 900-925.

5. Parvati Temple (AD 950-1000)

This temple, situated immediately to the southwest of the Viswanatha, is a heavily restored small shrine, originally comprising a sanctum and porch. The porch is completely lost and of the sanctum, only the plinth has survived.

The doorway belongs to a Vaishnava shrine as is indicated by a Vishnu figure on the middle of the lintel, while the image in the sanctum represents

The monolithic sculpture of Nandi Bull opposite Vishwanath Temple

Gauri with the godha (iguana) as her vehicle. Near it, facing the main road, is a hundred-year old temple built by a Maharaja of Chhatarpur.

6. Lakshmana Temple (c. AD 930-950)

Lakshmana temple stands in the heart of a large cluster of temples near Shiv Sagar. This temple is the earliest and best preserved of the mature Chandella temples. It is dedicated to the triple-headed four-armed Vaikuntha form of Vishnu. The temple is attributed to King Yasoverman. An inscribed slab, which was originally excavated at the base of the temple, is now fixed in the passageway around the sanctum.

The main temple is built on a high platform terrace and is surrounded by four subsidiary shrines. The four subsidiary shrines are placed at the corners of the platform-terrace a fifth one, facing the entrance, may have originally been dedicated to Garuda, but enshrines now an image of Brahmani, locally called Devi. Although the Kandariya Mahadeva and Vishvanatha temples are also of the Panchayatana (five-shrines) type, only the Lakshmana temple preserves all four-corner shrines. The subsidiary shrines, which have only a single curvilinear shaft, are smaller and simpler than the principal temple, but they also incorporate carved panels and ornamented doorways.

The entrance is by imposing steps, which run up the middle of the east side. Friezes on the terrace basement depict processions of horses, elephants, camels, battle scenes, dancers and musicians, domestic and erotic scenes, deities, ascetics with women, and ritualized sexual acts. Beautifully carved elephants at the base are built as if they were supporting the temple. The temple also has one of the finest specimens of Apsara brackets.

The temple is entered through an elegant two-looped Makara-torana (arch with carved crocodiles) flanked by gladiators. A pillared hall, at the corner of which are carved brackets with Apsaras, leads to the sanctum. Eight figures on each column represent the eight sects of Tantra.

The doorway of the sanctum is adorned with carvings and bands, which depict lions, Vishnu incarnations (as a fish, tortoise, boar and his composite form with a central human head flanked by boar and lion heads), the Navagrahas (nine planetary deities including Chandra, Surya, Mangala and Rahu) and on the doorjamb are reliefs depicting the Sagar Manthan or Churning of the ocean. The sanctum is Panch-ratha (five projections) and enshrines an image of Vishnu as Vaikuntha. Two bands of carved panel, depicting Apsaras and surasundaris in the projections and couples in complicated sexual acts in the recesses cover the exterior walls of the passageway below the main tower. The Apsaras and surasundaris are in attendance to the deities, bearing offerings, dancing or playing musical instruments, dressing or wringing out their wet hair. The additional porches are separated by balconies and angled eaves.

The best examples of medieval art adorn the Jangha (walls), those of a pair of minstrels, their faces expressing devotional rapture, and a dancing Ganesha on the southern façade are among the finest.

7. Vishvanatha Temple (AD 1002)

Vishvanatha temple is built near a ruined tank called Dhugavan. This temple is dedicated to Shiva in his aspect as Lord of the Universe. According to an inscribed slab now in the temple porch, King Dhangadeva built this temple. It anticipates the Kandariya Mahadeva which marks the culmination of the Chandella style, but is laid out in much the same manner as the Lakshmana temple which predates it, introducing subtle variations in the main shrine-the basement has smaller niches, doubled in two tiers. Only two out of four subsidiary shrines are intact i.e. in northeast and southwest corner.

The outer façade has the traditional three broad bands of sculpture. The high basement on the terrace has fine scrollwork, carvings of processions of men and animals, and amorous couples. The basement niches are carved with the Saptamatrikas (seven Mothers) with Ganesha and Virabhadra.

A richly adorned doorway provides access to the sanctuary, which originally had an emerald linga

in addition to the present one enshrined in the sanctuary. Within the temple, the main hall and passageway around the shrine contain some of the loveliest sculptures, including one of a woman with a fruit in one hand and a parrot in the other, a mother with her child, amorous couples, a surasundari playing the flute and another, notable for her charming expression, painting her foot. The ceiling has elaborate patterns of many petalled flowers and hanging stamens. East of the temple, sharing its raised platform, is an open pavilion housing a large Nandi image; the basement has a frieze of elephants. The pavilion has a pyramidal roof of horizontal elements.

8. Nandi Shrine

This is a detached Nandi pavilion forming an integral part of the architectural scheme of the Vishvanath temple. The two temples stand facing each other on a common terrace, which is approached by lateral flights of steps, the southern steps being flanked by a pair of elephants and

A colossal monolithic image of boar incarnation of Lord Vishnu in the Varaha Temple

design, dimensions and decorative scheme this temple closely resembles the Jagadambi and consists of a sanctum without ambulatory, vestibule, maha-mandapa with lateral transepts and entrance-porch, the last being completely restored above the original plinth.

The main image enshrined in the sanctum represents an impressive sculpture of standing Surya driving in a chariot of seven horses. Three similar but smaller figures of Surya are depicted on the lintel of the ornate doorway. The temple walls are also carved with some of the finest figures of Sura-sundaris, erotic couples and gods including an eleven-headed Vishnu (in the central niche of the south façade) with the central head of Vishnu and the remaining heads representing the ten incarnations.

This temple is also known as Bharatji's temple. It measures 74'9" by 51'9". The technique of 'adorning the waste of shrine with bands of sculptural griddle' just as in the Lakshman temple has been followed in this temple also. The exterior

A colossal shiva-lingam in Matangeshwar Temple.

northern by a pair of lions. This shrine enshrines a powerful colossal image of Nandi, the bull vehicle of Shiva, which faces the main deity, of the Vishvanatha temple. The temple is 31'3" × 30'90" and the statue is 7'3" long & 6' high.

It is an open square pavilion resting on twelve pillars with a shallow two-pillared bay projecting from the middle of each side, the whole enclosed by a low parapet of plain kakshasana balustrade. It has a pyramidal roof of receding tiers of pidhas with an almost plain circular ceiling of overlapping course. The only noteworthy decoration on its facades is a bold elephant frieze on the basement resembling that of the Lakshmana temple.

9. Chitragupta Temple (early 11th century)

This is the only local temple dedicated to Surya (Sun God) and is situated about 91 m to the north of the Jagadambi temple and 183 m south-east of an ancient (Chandella) three-storied stepped tank, known as the chopra. In respect of plan,

Holy feet of Goddess Prithvi (Bhudevi) Varaha Temple.

walls are full of rich exquisite carvings. The figures on the plinth friezes are that of hunting scenes, elephant fights, processions, dancing girls etc.

10. Devi Jagadambi Temple (early 11th century)

The Devi Jagadambi temple shares a platform with the Kandariya Mahadeva temple. Originally dedicated to Vishnu, the image within the sanctum is one of Parvati as goddess of the world; this is not the original image but dates to the same period as the temple. It faces east. The plan of the temple is identical with that of Chitragupta temple. It is 73 ft. long and 42 ft. wide. Since the image is painted black, the temple is also known as Kali Temple. The image of Vishnu carved so prominently on the Lalatabimba or the sanctum doorway that it refers to, as if the temple was originally dedicated to Vishnu.

Its basement-mouldings, however are simple and are devoid of the processional frieze-a conspicuous feature of the Chitragupta temple. Again unlike the Chitragupta, which has six

The image of Jain Tirthankara Parshwanath, Shantinatha Temple.

The image of Dakshinmurti Shiva in triple flexure in Chaturbhuj Temple.

pairs of dvara-palas disposed all round the maha-mandapa interior, this temple shows only three pairs of them.

The square ceiling of its maha-mandapa hall is much simpler than the octagonal ceiling of the Chitragupta temple, which thus appears to be relatively more ornate and evolved and therefore slightly later in date than this temple.

The carvings on the outer walls are among the best. They include several of Vishnu, one of Yama (the God of death), amorous couples and surasundaris whose sinuous postures and expressions of intense absorption characterize them as masterpieces of the fully developed Chandella style. It is perhaps the most erotic temple of Khajuraho.

11. Ruined Shiva Temple (11th Century)

On the same platform, between the Kandariya and the Jagadambi temples is a much smaller but ruined Shiva temple, as is indicated by a figure of Shiva carved centrally on the lintel of the

Clockwise from top: Vishwanath Temple, dedicated to Shiva; Parshwanath Temple; Nandi Temple; Chaturbhuj Temple has noteworthy sculptures but it has no erotic descriptions.

Clockwise from top: Devi Jagdambi Temple has erotic poses of rare sensitiveness; Vishwanath Temple; an overview of Jain Temples, Eastern Group; Chitragupta Temple, dedicated to the sun god, Surya.

Devi Jagdambi Temple, dedicated to Kali, was built in c. AD 1000 during the reign of Dhangadeva (c. 954-1002).

sanctum-doorway. The sanctum has perished, but the portico is intact and shelters now a powerful figure of shardula and a crouching female figure.

12. Kandariya Mahadeva Temple (c. 1025-50)

This is the largest, loftiest and the finest among the existing Khajuraho temples having a plinth area of 102'3" by 66'10" and standing 101'9" in height. Originally Kandariya temple was a panchayatan type temple, but four subsidiary shrines at the four corners of the terrace do not exist now.

The six main parts of a full fledged Khajuraho temple, viz. the Ardha mandapa, Mandapa, Mahamandapa, Antarala, Garbhagriha and Pradakshina path are co-ordinated here into an integrated whole. The roof of each of these parts designed as a mountain peak comprising of Amalaka and Kalas. From Sculpture and architecture point of view, Kandariya is considered to be the best temple among the Khajuraho group of temples. It looks like a mountain of masonry with shikharas appearing

like peak upon peak. Eighty-four smaller projections are carried upwards to the shikhara in a great sweep resulting in a superstructure, which is visually somewhat restless but unified. The graded hall roofs and shikhara signify the mythical Mount Kailash in the Himalayas. The layout affects the shape and architectural appearance of the exterior, which is an effective combination of bold projections and recesses, the whole being held together by horizontal bands of carvings. The temple is approached by a flight of stairs. At the entrance the artistic arch (torana) is decorated with figures of deities, Mithunas, musicians, kirtimukhas, makaras etc. Kandariya is the only local temple, which displays two makaratoranas, both of exquisite design, in the interior. The ceiling of the Ardhamandapa and Mandapa are carved richly. The ceiling of the mahamandapa composed of concentric overlapping circles. The lintels of the sanctum and the doorjambs have rich floral carvings. The figures of Ganga and Yamuna on their respective

Kandariya Mahadev Temple is architecturally and structurally the quintessential temple at Khajuraho.

Vahana, the makara (crocodile) and kurma (tortoise) are carved on the bases of the doorjambs. Inside the sanctum, a square chamber, stands a marble linga, the phallic symbol of Shiva.

Eight hundred sculptures are carved on its interior and exterior walls. The sculptures on this temple are conspicuously slender and taller and show the richest variety of Apsaras-types in lively and often violently agitated postures. Exhibiting mastery in the rendering of female contours and revealing a peak of conscious sophistication and exuberant grace, these sculptures represent the highest watermark of the characteristic art-diction of Khajuraho. Three bands of sculpture on the outer walls depict gods and goddesses including aspects of Shiva, dikpalas, maithunas and surasundaris in the projections interspersed with mythical beasts in the recesses. Apsaras in a variety of alluring positions are particularly notable for their slender form. The erotic sculptures are concentrated on the northern and southern façade, in the juncture between the shrine and the main hall. The roof of the mandapa is also intricately carved and the basement is provided with processional friezes that illustrate courtly themes.- Warriors and hunters, acrobats, musicians, dancers, devotees and amorous couples. Niches in the basement house figures of goddesses carved almost all around.

The Eastern Group

The eastern group of monuments, situated in close proximity to the Khajuraho village, includes three more Brahmanical temples known as the Brahma, Vamana and Javari, and three Jaina temples, the Ghantai, Adinatha and Parsvanatha. The Brahmanical temples are located along or near the Khajuraho sagar, while the Jaina temples are situated farther south and are conveniently approached by a metalled road.

1. Brahma Temple (c. AD 900)

This temple with a simple plan and design and with sikhara made of sandstone and the body of granite, occupies a fine position on the bank of the

The apsara discards her lower garments; scorpion on her thigh denotes passion, Devi Jagdambi Temple.

Khajuraho-sagar or Ninora-tal. It is miscalled Brahma on account of a four-faced linga now enshrined in the sanctum, but must have originally been dedicated to Vishnu as shown by his figure carved centrally on the sanctum-doorway.

It is a modest structure, comprising a sanctum and a porch, the latter now completely lost and the former rooted by a pyramidal sikhara of receding tiers of pidhas, crowned by a prominent bell-member. The sanctum is cruciform externally with projection on each side, and square internally, resting on twelve plain pilasters of granite. The projection on the east contains the entrance and that on the west is pierced with a smaller doorway, while the lateral projections on the remaining two sides contain plain-latticed windows.

Except for the boldly modeled figures of the Brahmanical Trinity on the lintel and of Ganga and Yamuna at the base, its doorway is plain. Its jangha (wall) divided into two registers and standing on simple difference in details, this temple belongs to the same conception and early

structural phase as the Lalguan-Mahadeva, with which it shares a common plan, design, ornaments and building material. It is consequently assignable to circa 900.

2. Statue of Hanuman

A colossal statue of Hanuman, the monkey-god, is housed in a modern shrine situated about halfway between the western group of temples and the Khajuraho village. It is interesting mainly on account of a short dedicatory inscription on its pedestal, dated 316 of possibly the Harsha era (A.D. 922), being the oldest dated inscription at the place.

3. Vamana Temple (c. AD 1050-75)

The Vamana temple is dedicated to Vishnu who in his fifth incarnation is said to have taken the form of a dwarf (Vamana) and tricked the demon Bali into granting him as much land as he could cover in three strides. The dwarf became a giant, strode the universe in three strides and staked his claim from Bali, thus depriving the latter of his domain. The temple, which is an example of the

A surasundari applying 'sindoor', Lakshmana Temple.

54

fully evolved Chandella style, has a shikhara without clustered elements and no ambulatory. The shikhara rises in bands that continue the projections of the walls beneath. These bands are covered with a grid of arch-like patterns; the summit is surmounted by an amalaka and pot-finial. The outer walls have only two bands of sculptures, which include sensuous surasundaris, many of which are damaged, but erotic sculptures do not feature here. In sanctum wall the image of Buddha in Bhoomisparsha Mudra has been carved while main niches of the sanctums contains the figures of Brahma, Vishnu and Shiva with their consorts. A richly carved doorway leads to the sanctum, which houses the 4'5" high image of the four-armed Vamana.

4. The Shantinath temple

This is a modern Jain temple located at the south of Parshwanath. 14 ft. high image of Jain Tirthankar Rishabhdev is the important figure. A bull is carved on the pedastal of the image. The temple includes a few other ancient sculptures of

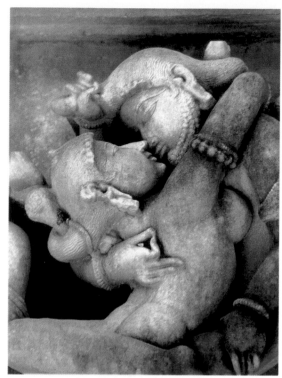

An erotic couple, Vishwanath Temple.

Jain Gods and Goddesses.

5. The Parshwanath Temple (mid-10th century)

This belongs to Jain group of temples and is one of the important temples in Khajuraho. It is said to have been originally dedicated to Adinath, the Jain Tirthankar. The present image of Parshwanath was installed in 1860 A.D. The temple is oblong in shape and it measures 68 ft. by 35 ft. It has two axial projections at the east and west. In the east is Ardhmandapa and at west behind the sanctum is a small shrine. It is a 'Sandhara Prasada' and has a ambulatory passage. Entrance porch has ornate ceiling containing five pendants. This is situated between the temples of Adinath and Shantinath. On the outer walls there are bands of lavishly carved figures. All these figures have been carved with wonderful artistic skill and aesthetic splendour. The images belong to both Vaishnava as well as Jaina. Notable among the figures in this temple are ten armed Chakreswari, Parasuram, Balaram-Revati, Rama-Sita and Hanuman. Some

A surasundari taking bath, Lakshmana Temple.

Shiva with his consort Parvati, Duladeo Temple.

Kama with his consort Rati, Parshwanath Temple.

of the figures such as that of nayika writing a letter, a damsel extracting a thorn, a woman fondling a child etc. are among the famous sculptural figures of the Khajuraho temples.

6. The Adinath Temple (late 11th century)

The temple is dedicated to the Jain Tirthankar Adinath. The statue of the dJeity, which was originally installed in the sanctum, is missing and another statue of Adinath is installed. This is a small temple of three chambers of which vestibule and sanctum has survived. In general, design and elegance of sculptural style it resembles the Vamana temple. But Shikhara is lighter and more proportionate than in Vamana. The three bands of carvings around the walls depict Hindu Gods and Goddesses, elegant celestial beauties, flying Vidyadharas etc. The sculptures also include some nude figures of females and attractive dancing girls and Apsaras.

7. The Ghantai Temple (late 10th century)

This is also one of the Jain Group of temples. It was named after the 'bell and chain' ornaments carved in the pillars; Much of the temple has been ruined and there now remain only the roof and elegant pillars decorated with Kirtimukhas from whose mouth hang the festoons of pearls and bells which, of course, present a splendid illustration of sculptural art. At the entrance of the temple is a image of an eight armed Jain Goddess riding a Garuda and flourishing various weapons, Doorway carvings depict the sixteen dreams of the mother of Mahavira and nine planets. It resembles Parshwanath Temple in plan and design.

8. The Javari Temple (c. AD 1075-1100)

The architectural design of this small temple is magnificent. This stands on the lofty terrace, Nirandhra Prasada type, that is without ambulatory path and on the outer walls there are three bands of sculpture. It measures 39 ft. by 21 ft. and consists of Ardhamandapa (Portico), Mahamandapa and the sanctum. The decoration of the portico and assembly hall is done by exquisite proportionate carvings. The sanctum is enshrined with fourhanded (Chaturbhuj) image of Vishnu. The rising spire adds additional charm to the structure.

The Southern Group

The southern group of monuments comprises the Duladeo and the Chaturbhuja or Jatkari temple.

1. Duladeo Temple (c. AD 1100-50)

The Duladeo temple, also called Kunwar Math (meaning holy bridegroom, a reference to Shiva) standing south of the Ghantai temple was built on the north bank of the Khudar Nala. It is notable for being the latest temple of Khajuraho. Dedicated to Shiva, it is a nirandhara temple and consists of a sanctum, vestibule, maha-mandapa and porch. Its shikara is of the usual developed form, clustered round by three tows of minor shikaras, its maha-mandapa hall is remarkable large and octagonal showing twenty Apsaras-brackets, grouped in bunches of two of three,

abutting against its corbelled circular ceiling.

While the dancing Apsaras of its interiors and the flying Vidyadharas on the top rows of its facades show overburdened with ornamentation. While some figures on this temple are of an exceptional artistic merit, the plastic treatment has, on the whole, become fluid and, in many cases, lacks depth of relief, which is evident on a majority of the Apsaras-figures of the exterior. The iconography of this temple also shows some distinctive traits. The Ashtavasu figures are invariably depicted here with a crocodile-mount in place of the usual bull, while Yama and Nritti, two of the Dikpalas, wear their raised curls in a stylized fan shape. Thus, plastically and iconographically, the temple marks the exhaustion of the remarkable vitality for which the Khajuraho sculptures are justly famous, and its peculiarities, both sculptural and architectural, are such that it could be placed only at the end of the finer series of the Khajuraho temples.

Erotic scene, north wall of uppermost row, Kandariya Mahadev Temple

Mithun couple, Devi Jagdambi Temple

An erotic scene on the northern wall of Vishwanath Temple

2. Chaturbhuja Temple (early 11th century)

This is the farthest temple, situated about 3 km south of Khajuraho and 600m southwest of Jatkari village. It is a Nirandhara temple of a modest size similar to the Javari, and consists on plan of a sanctum carrying a simple shikara of heavy proportions, vestibule, mandapa and a porch. This is the only developed local temple that lacks erotic sculptures. The sanctum enshrines a colossal fourhanded image of Chaturbhuja Vishnu to whom the temple is dedicated. So-called Dakshinamurti (South facing image) faces west. The image is 10 ft. 3 inches high and decorated with crown and other ornaments. According to locals, this single image held the crown of Shiva, the face of Buddha, the body of Vishnu and the stance of Krishna. The Shikhara is of curvilinear type and has no turrets. The noteworthy piece of carving is a lion-headed female on the north, which is perhaps the female counterpart of Narsingh the man-lion incarnation of Vishnu. Ardha-nariswara image of Shiva is another important sculpture in this temple.

Archaeological Museum

The museum lies near the entrance to the Western group of temples, and contains near 2,000, 10th-11th century sculptures retrieved over fifty years from the site. The entrance to the museum is a temple doorway. Among the finest exhibits are a large dancing Ganesha figure (c. AD 1130) which stands in the entrance hall, a panel depicting two tirthankaras (c. AD 1635) and a standing Surya figure surrounded by miniature attendants (c. AD 1262). In the Vaishnava gallery are numerous sculptures of the various incarnations of Vishnu; among them is one of Varaha (c. AD 861). Seated images of Buddha (c. AD 450) and a five-headed Shiva (c. AD 1098) are also displayed. Though remains of temples belonging to the Khajuraho group have been discovered at Jatkari, 3 km away and even at Maribag in Rewa, it is at the 3 main groups that the imperishable glory of Khajuraho, the sensuous celebration of life, the aspiration towards the infinite, remains.

Clockwise form top left: Image of Jain Tirthankra Parshwanath, Shantinath Temple; Western Group of Temples; Kandariya Mahadev Temple; bell and chain motifs carved on the tall pillars of the Ghantai Temple; shopping area at Khajuraho; Lakshamana Temple with corner shrines viewed from south-east.

Orchha

Orchha is one of the medieval city built during 16th century by Bundel Rajput Chieftain Rudrapratap on the banks of rocky Betwa river in Bundelkhund region of Madhya Pradesh. It is situated on Jhansi-Khajuraho road, 170 km from Khajuraho and 16 km from Jhansi. Bir Singh Ju Deo, the successor of Rudrapratap developed the city during 17th century and what it is today is a memorable rich legacy of the ages that attracts many tourists. The very word "Orchha" means "hidden" and, verily, the small town of Orchha in Madhya Pradesh (India) stands for it. It is a hidden archaeological legacy of medieval India, it is a hidden 'throb' of romance and emotional rupture, it is a hidden face of history, a hidden treasure of spiritual tranquility, a hidden poetry written on stones.

Orchha is located in northern part of the state of Madhya Pradesh, in the central region of India. It lies beside the Malwa plateau. The Betwa River flows through the town. The climate of Orchha is temperate. Summers (April-June) are not too hot while winters are cool (November-February) and pleasant. It experiences southwestern monsoon rains in July-September. The best time to visit Orchha is between October and March.

Blood, war and sacrifice are the keywords to describe the Rajput Bundela dynasty that ruled over Orchha for over two centuries beginning from 1531 A.D. This developed as a stronghold of Rajput power in India and as a symbol of love and valor. It is said that there was a Rajput prince who intended to offer himself as a sacrifice to Vindhyavasini the goddess of the Vindhya hills. The goddess was glad with his devotional attitude and named him 'Bundela' which means "the offerer of the drops (of blood)". However true or untrue this story be, it is true that 'sacrifice' is the very essence of a Bundela life and the Rajput history of India amply testifies this fact. Orchha has witnessed lots of ups and downs of time. The history of Orchha is linked with the local Bundela rulers. It has a chequered history. The Bundela dynasty was founded by one of the local Rajput princes in the 11th century. Garkhurar was the earlier capital of the Bundelas. The Bundelas ruled the central part of India from Orchha, from 1531 to 1783. Raja Rudra Pratap moved the capital of the Bundelas to Orchha in 1531.

The association of the Bundelas with the Mughals created many problems for the Bundelas. Bir

Chattris across river Betwa. 15 memorials to the rulers of Orchha are grouped along the Kanchana ghat of the river.

Top left: Chaturbhuj Temple houses an idol of Lord Rama **Top right:** Jahangir Mahal, built by Raja Bir Singh Ju Deo (17th century) **Bottom left:** One of the 15 chattris **Bottom right:** The town of Orchha as seen from the Raj Mahal.

Jahangir Mahal is five-storied and houses 8 pavilions.

Singh Deo, the ruler of Orchha from 1605-27, got into serious trouble with the great Mughal Emperor Akbar in 1602, when he was associated with Prince Jahangir, the son of Emperor Akbar. Mughal forces all but destroyed the state of the Bundelas. However, the situation changed in 1605, when Akbar died and Jahangir became the Mughal Emperor. In 1606, Emperor Jahangir visited Orchha. For the next 22 years until 1627, Bir Singh Deo had good relations with the Mughals. In 1627, when Shahjahan became the Mughal Emperor, Bir Singh revolted against the Mughals. However, Aurangzeb put down this revolt, the 13-year old son of Shahjahan. Though the Mughals defeated the Bundelas, they revived their lost empire. In 1783, the Bundela rulers shifted their capital to Tikamgarh.

Orchha is most famous for its beautiful fort. Palaces (mahals), temples, gardens and cenotaphs (chhatris-memorials) also dot its landscape. The Bundela School of painting known for its finest flowering art is one main reason to visit Orchha. This ancient city has a lot to offer to the tourists. The main attraction of Orchha is the Orchha fort complex, located on an island on River Betwa, having a number of palaces to visit within it. A four-arched bridge leads to the fort complex on the island.

The Jahangir Mahal, which was built by Bir Singh Deo in the early part of the 17th century to mark the visit of the Mughal Emperor, is an important monument of this fort. The 70 m square palace has a smaller interior courtyard with a central

fountain around which are apartments and terraces in three storeys. A dome caps each corner bastion. Hanging balconies with wide eaves run along the exterior walls and are counterbalanced by delicate chhatris and trelliswork, making for an effect of extraordinary richness. Windows and terraces overlook the Betwa River on the banks of which are the memorial cenotaphs of the Orchha kings. About half of the fifteen royal chhatris, grouped on the Kanchana Ghat of the Betwa, are well preserved and appear to be etched against the evening sky, presenting a particularly enchanting sight. The interiors of the palace exhibit the finest specimen of the Bundela School of painting. Within the fort are also numerous shrines, memorials and monuments. The architecture is a hybrid of traditional Hindu and elaborate Mughal. Raj Mahal, the second palace in this fort complex is well known for its murals, depicting religious themes. The deeply religious Madhukar Shah built it between 1554 and 1591. Its plain exterior, a solid single block crowned by chhatris (umbrella-like memorial cenotaphs), gives way to the royal chambers in which exquisite murals from Hindu mythology line the walls and ceilings.

Rai Praveen Mahal was built for the beautiful paramour of Raja Indramani (1672-76), who was a poetess and a musician. Perveen was a beautiful lady of her time with great artistic taste and abilities. She was a superb dancer as well as a singer. The dales of Orchha ring with the stories of Jehangir's romance with her. Jehangir loved her deeply and wanted to marry her an offer that she refused. The Palace of Raj Perveen is, thus, not only a monument of romance but also of an Indian queen's faithfulness to her husband. It is a low two-storey brick structure, designed so as to match the height of the trees in the surrounding, beautifully landscaped gardens of Anand Mahal, with its octagonal flower beds and elaborate water supply system. Skillfully carved niches allow light into the Mahal, which has a main hall and smaller chambers. The palace of Hardaul is another important monument of romance. Hardaul was the son of Bir Singh Ju Deo, and died to prove his innocence to his elder brother Jhujhar who cast doubts on his relationship with his (Jhujhar's) consort. This saintly prince was, after his martyrdom, worshipped as a god and even today, the villages of Bundelkhand contain platform like shrines where Hardaul is worshipped.

Singh Ju Deo, and died to prove his innocence to his elder brother Jhujhar who cast doubts on his relationship with his (Jhujhar's) consort. This saintly prince was, after his martyrdom, worshipped as a god and even today, the villages of Bundelkhand contain platform like shrines where Hardaul is worshipped. The Ram Raja Temple, also within the fort, was originally a palace but turned into a temple with its soaring spires and palatial architecture. The legend goes that Rani Ganesh Kunwari, wife of Madhukar Shah, brought a statue of Lord Rama from Ayodhya to Orchha to install it in a temple. It was kept temporarily in the palace. When the idol had to be shifted for installation it was impossible to move it. Finally, it was decided to consecrate it in the palace itself. It is the only temple in the country where Ram is worshipped as a Raja (king), probably because the statue of the god is in a palace.

The Chaturbhuj Temple, reached by a steep flight of steps, was built by Madhukar Shah for his queen Kunwari. Laid out in the form of a cross on a large stone platform, it has delicate exterior ornamentation with lotus emblems and religious symbols. A tall shikhara (spire) rises over the sanctum, which is chastely plain with high walls emphasizing its sanctity. A stone path links the Ram Raja Temple to the Lakshminarayana Temple, which fuses elements of fort architecture in temple moulds. The interiors contain some of the most exquisite murals and wall paintings of the Bundela School of painting.

Phool Bagh is laid out as a formal garden, this complex testifies to the refined aesthetic qualities of the Bundelas. A central row of fountains culminates in an eight-pillared palace-pavilion. A subterranean structure below was the cool summer retreat of the Orchha kings. An ingenious system of water ventilation connects the underground palace with Chandan Katora, a bowl-like structure from whose fountains droplets

of water flittered through to the roof, simulating rainfall. Shahid Smarak (martyrs' Memorial), which commemorates the freedom fighter Chandrashekhar Azad who lived in Orchha in 1926-27, now houses a library and museum.

Another small palace, Sunder Mahal, now almost in ruins, is still a place of sanctity for Muslims. It belonged to the grandson of Bir Singh Deo, Dhurbjan, who embraced Islam after he married a Muslim girl and spent the latter part of his life in prayer. He came to be venerated as a saint and his palace became a revered site of pilgrimage. The Chhatris or cenotaphs, the memorial of the rulers of Bundels, is situated near the Kanchan Ghat on River Betwa laid in a row of 14, present a wonderful sight which some also find eerie. The shrines of Siddh Baba ka Sthan, the Jugal Kishore Mandir and Janaki Mandir are also worth seeing. Today, Orchha is a remote village with a population of no more than a few thousand. Rarely visited, it is a haven of tranquility and the route leading to it through forested and gently undulating countryside is very attractive. Its monuments are the blended mixture of Rajasthani, Jain and Mugal architecture traditions, which draw many tourists. The blending gives the monuments of Orchha a unique value as well as a distinctive aesthetic expression. Hosts of temples, chhatris and shrines reflect an archaeologically rich legacy of time referred to by some historians as "medieval legacy in stone".

A part of Orchha's fort complex which has 3 palaces set in an open quadrangle.

Excursions

Though the temples of Khajuraho are a powerful lure, there are several places of interest near Khajuraho worth visiting.

Ajaygarh Fort (61 km from Khajuraho via Panna, 26 km from Kalanjar) : This fort, built in the 9th century by the Chandella kings, stands at a height of 688 m on a granite outcrop. Of the five main gates only two are now accessible. An outer rampart encircles the hill and is studded with ruins of ancient Hindu sculptures and carvings which were used by the Muslims to reinforce the fortifications. In 1809, the British Indian Army bombarded the fort after a local chief, Lakshman Daowa, defied them, the barrage remains where it fell, now encroached by teak and ebony forests.

Data (192 km from Khajuraho) : Datia finds mention in the epic, Mahabharata. The seven-storey Nrising Dev Palace (Govind Mandir), the cenotaphs of the former ruling family, a temple with Mughal frescoes and the Gopeshwar temple are places of historical interest. Nrising Dev Palace, built by Raja Bir Singh Deo (c. 1620), is regarded as one of the finest examples of domestic architecture. Along with the palace at Orchha, it is the best surviving specimen of 16th and 17th century architecture that developed under the Bundela Rajputs. The southern side of the palace overlooks a large lake, the Karna Sagar. Datia is worth visiting.

Jhansi (158 km from Khajuraho) : Jhansi is best known for its fine fort and its legendary queen, Lakshmi Bai, a heroine of the Indian Mutiny of 1857, who died fighting the British. The fort was built by Raja Bir Deo in 1613, with concentric walls, 5.5-9 m high and ten gates. The British breached the wall between Sainyar and Jhirna gates during the assault of 1858. The city extends beyond the old wall which has been modernized. Rani Mahal, once Lakshmi Bai's home, is now a museum. Retribution Hill, northeast of the railway station, marks the last stand of the rebels in the mutiny.

Kalanjar Fort (100 km from Khajuraho) : One of the most ancient sites in Bundelkhand, Kalanjar was a venerated hill shrine (sanctified as the abode of Lord Shiva) for Hindu sadhus and pilgrims long before it was fortified and occupied by successive invaders. The fort stands on the last spur of the Vindhya hills overlooking the Gangetic plains. It is believed to have been built during the Gupta period (AD 3rd-5th) before being captured by the Chandella ruler, Yasovarman, in the middle of the 10th century. The only approach is from the north, through seven gates, the names of which correspond to the seven stations through which the soul is believed to pass before being integrated with Brahma, the Absolute, Beyond the last gate is a drop of 3.6 m leading to Sita Sej, a stone couch set in a chamber carved from rock (4th century), and further ahead a passage leading to the Patalganga (underground river) which runs through the fort.

Panna National Park (32 km from Khajuraho) : Comprising 543 sq km of dense teak jungle over valleys and plateaux bordering the river Ken, Panna National Park is home to a variety of wildlife, including the tiger, panther, wolf, and also attracts a variety of birds. Paradise flycatchers, Madhya Pradesh's state bird, are found in profusion. There is also a gharial (crocodile) sanctuary in the vicinity of the spectacular Raneh falls.

Rajgarh (25 km north of Khajuraho) : Rajgarh has a majestic 150-year old hilltop palace. The sleepy village comes to life on Tuesdays when the local people gather here for the weekly market.

Shivpuri (293 km from Khajuraho) : The former summer capital of the Scindia rulers of Gwalior, Shivpuri has exquisite palaces, intricately carved marble chhatris and hunting lodges. The Sakhia Sagar and Madhav Sagar lakes are surrounded by the Madhav National Park (160 sq km of deciduous forest) which is home to the tiger, leopard, deer, wild dog and sloth bear. The lakes harbour the Indian crocodile. In the nearby Karera Bird Sanctuary, one can find the Great Indian Bustard, once on the brink of extinction.